CONVERSATIONS
WITH RACHAEL

CONVERSATIONS WITH RACHAEL

My Guardian Angel

KENNETH BARBB

Conversations With Rachael
My Guardian Angel

Cover Art by Kenneth Barbb

Copyright © 2016 by Kenneth Barbb

ISBN: 9780966560640
ISBN: 0966560647
Library of Congress Control Number: 2016914572
Lockport Enterprizes, Holland, MI
Revised 2017

DEDICATION

To all who believe, and those who need something in which
to believe.

THANKS AND APPRECIATION

To those who encouraged me throughout this journey I must say
thank you, you are true friends. To Loretta Layne who helped keep
my mind going and always questioning. To Myron Kukla, author
Guide to Surviving Life, all your help is very much appreciated. Thank
you Teresa Skupinski, longtime friend and author, and Kendyl Layne
for editing. To Marilynn Voss, thank you for questioning my wording. Last I would like to thank my wife Mary Jo for giving me the
determination to carry out the writing of these conversations.

INTRODUCTION

Never in my wildest thoughts or dreams would I have envisioned what you are about to experience.

Guardian angels. I always believed that one day I would meet him, or in my case her. Throughout life many paths are meant to be crossed. This crossing was a long time in coming, but well worth the wait. I repeatedly have asked to meet my guardian angel, or angels in my dreams. Then one night it happened.

CONTENTS

CHOICES

Throughout life we make many choices. Some turn out to be good, others not. As you read you have a choice to make. Do I believe or do I not believe? Please do not take offense if your thoughts or beliefs are different from mine. Offending is not my intention. All I ask is that you read with an open mind.

There is no rhyme or reason, no special order for the following exchanges. They are as they happened. A number of exchanges taking place when I was away from my recorder or computer. At those times relying on memory and being vigilant as to not change the wording or meaning of what was told me in answer. These are my thoughts, my conversations. My words, Rachael's words.

I write the words given, and hopefully many will take comfort in them. I believe nothing is impossible. It is from my mind and heart that I share these words. I believe what I believe and God is one of my beliefs. Many may believe as I do, many may not. Some may believe in a higher power, or a universal power, or whatever name they care to use. Some may not; it's their choice.

So relax, take a deep breath and enjoy the following.

IT BEGINS

(Mid to late June)

Rachael, why is it I never knew of you before this time?

I believe Kenneth that now was the right time for you to remember me, not sooner. It is time for additional learning.

Remember you? You say this as if we have known each other for some time. Additional learning?

This I say, and yes we have. You will learn what it is you need to know when you need to know. I have known you since you were a thought in creation. I have known your soul from the time it was envisioned and came into being. I have been your guardian since before your forever. You have known me; you just don't remember our meeting. We are soul mates; now the time is right to reconnect.

Whoa! This whole conversation is freaking me out. I recently met you and you lay this on me like it's an every day occurrence?

Be calm, trust in me. I am now and always have been here to watch over and protect you. I can help guide you if you like. Just trust me.

ALL IS WELL

I was formed in the great beyond,
not in body, but in thought,
this happened before forever.

My mind is that of the universe,
always expanding, always learning,
a great mystery.

My eyes shimmer as if stars,
my voice sounds, as does the thunder,
my heart beats as the oceans ebb and flow.

My spirit moves like the wind,
fresh and free,
my being is in control.

I was formed from the dust
of the earth,
from flesh and bone,
I was formed from love.

All is well.

QUESTIONS

Rachael, there are so many things I want to ask you. Will you answer all my questions? May I please write about our conversations?

I will tell you what I will tell you. There are answers you don't need at this time, they will be answered in due time. As for telling about this I say "no", and I say it softly.

Why not?

Many won't believe you. You've been around long enough to know how people think.

Do you think we should ever tell? I think some people will believe and understand what's being said.

Believe me many won't. They will doubt you and your motive.

Why do you say that? Is it that people will think I possess an overactive imagination, or that I'm making up this whole conversation? Will they doubt my motive?

People will think what they will think no matter what. It is how it is. Many have lost their way and so many have given up in believing anything is possible.

Lost their way? Given up on what?

Life, love and truth just to name a few. True love, not the love that many profess, the empty words. They have lost faith in their fellow man. They have been deceived and are blinded and no longer see what is and what was good. They have given up on God.

Are you sure, do you really believe that?

Yes I do. I know it in my heart.

You say they've given up, but why? Why have they given up?

Because of greed, lust and the loss of morals. They wander aimlessly as though they're lost in an abyss. They have lost hope, and without hope you have nothing.

That's sad.

Yes, very sad and I weep for them. I weep for them and for the world.

MAY I TELL?

Rachael, may I please tell about you? I feel many will benefit from knowing.

All right, but please be gentle as many are in a fragile state. This may be the opportune time for people to learn of our conversations. Hopefully this will help guide them back. We need them to regain what is needed to get them back to what is true and honest, kind and loving. Too many are being misguided. They are being blinded from what is and what needs to happen. We need them on our side.

On our side? Just what do you mean by that Rachael? It sounds ominous to me, like something is about to happen. Is that what you're saying? Are you trying to warn me, or scare me?

Don't be frightened. What I'm saying is mankind needs to get back to what is true; the right path needs to be traveled. There is time enough for this to be accomplished, but the healing needs to start soon

Thank you my sweet Rachael.

SORROW

(July 29th)

All of heaven is crying, as am I. I stood watching the rain hitting the window and this thought entered my mind, "All of heaven is crying. Each drop of water is a tear being shed," I said aloud. "All of heaven is crying for my beloved Sassy cat." For sixteen years she was at my side, and now she's gone. Today was a very hard day, a sad day indeed. I'm tired, as this loss has drained me. Rachael, I'm so sad.

I know my love; you will have her in you heart and thoughts forever until you come together again. And yes, you will be together again along with all others you love. Know that it will be. She may visit you in your dreams, or lay beside you purring as you sleep. Believe that love transcends death. Your cry of sorrow is heard. Heaven is crying tears of joy, as will you one day. She is now home again. Your sorrow will fade; now embrace your loss. All of heaven is crying with you.

Thank you Rachael. My heart feels love, but at this moment my heart feels sorrow, deep sorrow.

YOUR TRUTH

What you hold in your heart is your truth.

SOUL MATES

Let me back up a bit Rachael. We have had a relationship only recently known by me. From what you have told me you have known me much longer than I have known. Also, in one of our conversations you said you were my soul mate. I always thought that your soul mate was the person you married and/or went happily through life with. Am I wrong about this? Maybe you could expound on this for me.

Yes Kenneth, I did declare that we are soul mates, and we are, as you will see. I was there when your soul came into itself and I chose to be your guardian soul mate. Your guardian soul mate, not your life soul mate. Your life soul mate (if you are lucky enough to find them) is the one you marry or go through life with. As in your case it took some time to find your true earth soul mate, but not an unusual occurrence. There are different degrees of soul mates, some are here forever and others are here for a short time. Maybe it's to teach you a lesson that needs to be learned, or help advance your life without you even knowing. Some people never find their true soul mate for the simple fact their internal being, their depth, is not strong enough, or they just don't care to find that special someone. So you see my love, when I refer to you with such loving expressions, it is that I have been with you, as I said earlier, before your forever. I am your true guardian soul mate. I choose to love you. It is my choice as I, as well as you, have free will to choose as I please. We will be together always, forever. It never ends. I hope that helps you understand.

I guess I understand. And when my time here ends, what then? Will I meet you and travel through eternity with you?

You will again meet me if you choose to do so. I will always be with you through all your future journeys. Do you remember meeting me in your dream? You were surprised that I am of golden hair, and not dark of hair. I thought that was amusing.

Rachael, why would you say if I choose to meet you?

Remember, it all comes back to free will.

I understand, but now I choose to do so. And yes I recall that dream. I am somewhat disappointed, as I can't remember your face very well. The dream ended too soon, it happened so fast. Maybe you could visit my dreams again. Also, you mentioned my future journeys. It sounds as though you are talking about reincarnation, or do I not understand what you're saying?

That's a subject for another time Kenneth. But yes, reincarnation.

EVIL

Rachael, did God create evil? And if so, why?

God created the universe and everything that is good. Evil is a manifestation of the universal law of balance. It's akin to the ying and yang; you can't have one without the other. No day without night, no dark without light, and no wrong without right.

Men and woman are blessed with free will in all things. At times it may seem a curse. It is not, it's a blessing and in the end it's just that, free will, freedom of choice. It is up to each person to make their choice, whether it's right or wrong, it's still their choice. Just as there has always been evil, there is much evil in the world at this time. It's strong and its strength grows everyday. Be vigilant. It is said that one day all the forces of good will unite to crush this tide of evil.

Is it that simple?

(Slight chuckle) No, it's not that simple, but it's said in a way you would understand. Eventually you will truly understand the meaning of all that is all. One of your life lessons is patience, which you have learned well. So be patient a little longer and enjoy what is now, and what is you. Don't forget to keep working on procrastination.

I'll do my best. I have to believe there is more good than evil in this world.

Good outweighs evil and I will do my part to protect you against that, which is evil, but all must remain vigilant.

HAVE YOU ALWAYS BEEN?

I'm curious about something Rachael. When did you come into being and have you always been a guardian angel?

I am of the Creators creation. I am of the beginning and am of the end. I am a guardian of the true guardians of the first of time.

Thanks Rachael.

(A Rachael smile)

BIG BANG

The other day I heard something about the Big Bang Theory and was wondering if you could shed some light on the subject? Anything on evolution would also be appreciated.

Well Kenneth, as you may know or believe, all things were created. If, and I say if the Big Bang happened it was a creation, not a random event as many may profess it to be. As far as evolution, this also was a creation of our Creator. Everything was created, with the exception of one thing. Hard to understand I know, but trust my words, you will be led to the truth.

Wait; you don't know if the Big Bang Theory is just that, a theory? And what is the one thing that wasn't created that you speak of?

Even we guardians don't know everything. We know what's important in order to perform our given and loved task. Yes, we love our task, as it's a pleasure for us to carry it out. There are others much higher on knowledge levels that could answer your question. Not I. The only thing not created is our God (our Creator) as He (I say He for ease of understanding) has always been. Always is a hard concept to understand just as what's at the end of space? So I am unable to answer your question about the Big Bang. I will however say I'm so excited for you Kenneth, as you still have much to learn in your given time, but even more afterwards. I am happy for you my love.

A RACHAEL THOUGHT

There are things I know and things I know not. At times I answer your queries with the least of an answer. You do not need to know all; it is not yet time for your knowledge or understanding. I do not know all that you may request. There are things more important than what you at times inquire. They may seem important, but occupy your time with things of value. Be patient my dear Kenneth and trust in my words

LOVE OF CATS

Rachael, you know of my love for cats. You've seen it over the past forty-five or so years. Sissy cat will be my last one here. The pain of losing a sweet furry friend is just too difficult. It's been a week and poor Sissy cat keeps calling for her sister to no avail. They've been together since birth for the last sixteen years, now she's alone. She calls, at times her call is quite vocal, then she stops and looks around. I have also heard her quietly calling almost as if to say, "please answer." It's heartbreaking to see her roaming from room to room and not finding Sassy. So Rachael, no more cats for me, no more.

I understand my love.

IMPOSSIBLE

I can't remember what prompted this conversation or many others, but you know the question asked.

Yes I do, and nothing is impossible Kenneth, as you will one day learn. The possibilities are endless and beyond anything your mind could conceive. You cannot begin to imagine the next realm; it's more than wondrous. As an artist you will appreciate the infinite number and sounds of color. Yes Kenneth, color does have a sound, as well as an aroma. I remember when you heard the slightest sounds of the extraordinary existence beyond life on earth. You were on the verge of being consumed by the water at a tender age and were thrilled at what you thought. You heard the heavenly choir presenting their loving sounds to welcome you home, as you began to enter into the ever-expanding light. Do you remember?

I remember; how could I ever forget. It's imprinted into my memory. I remember everything you mentioned, floating into the light, no fear and feeling warm and safe. The light began as light yellow, expanding outward with white at its core, getting brighter, then the sound starting low and increasing in volume, the sound like "Ahhhhhhh." That's the only way I can describe it. That's when I thought, "Wow, I don't have to breath." The next thing I knew, a girl, (probably in her late teens), pulled me out of the water and back into this life and reality. Yes, I remember.

That my dear Kenneth was only a glimpse of entering into something more than you could ever believe. Words cannot describe the heavens that await all who believe.

AGAINST THE WIND

You know Rachael, at times it's so hard to stay upbeat and positive. Life and its events can at times drag you down; especially when you're not feeling up to par. It's like that Bob Seger song says, "I feel like I'm running against the wind."

Kenneth my love, life will be filled with ups and downs, you know that. You ride the high times and wait as the tough times ebb, washing away your woes with it. You always tell others to stay strong. Now I say, this is your time to stay strong. You know you always weather the storm. As with everything these times will pass, nothing on earth is forever. Nothing. Remember that.

A RACHAEL REFLECTION

A down day is not a bad thing per se. It is the opportune time to reflect on the past, not dwell, but reflect. It's a time to let your mind quiet itself and remember what you have accomplished, a time to dream of future possibilities. Remember that anything is possible, anything. A time to give thanks for what is, and what will be in future days. You once said, "I cannot change the past, I can only move forward." This is a new day, a day for you once again to move forward.

THE PAST

The past is past,

what's now will pass,

your future will pass.

Reflect the past,

savor the past.

FAMILY GUARDIANS

Another thing I must ask is, "Do we have family members as guardian angels?"

Of course. You must know that family members become guardians. They love protecting their loved ones and they can be very helpful in assisting at times.

Why would it be necessary if I have other guardian angels?

Notice I said assist. It is their way of showing the love they have for their special person. That earthly bond of love is never broken: not by death or the distance between. Their bond is forever until they again are together.

———————

NATURAL LIFE

Rachael, earlier I asked you for the definition of natural life. I'll explain later why I asked. You said you would inquire with the higher powers for their definition. What did they tell you?

Their answer was not to bother yourself with its meaning as it is not of importance.

But it is important, here's why. When I was thirty-eight years old this thought popped into my mind like a slap in the face: "Wow, I just hit the halfway point of my natural life." Pretty significant thought I would say. That's why I need to know.

And I say this to you Kenneth. I was informed this could very well be a leftover occurrence from a previous life, that's why it's not as important as you may think. Spend your allotted time on your now life.

Could very well be?

Another time Kenneth.

I thought this would be a significant event in my life, and once again the implication of reincarnation pops up. Do you not know the meaning of this thought?

The meaning of the thought is unknown to me. It is not for me to understand.

We need to have the reincarnation conversation soon.

Yes soon.

MORNING

Sissy is quiet this morning, unlike the previous mornings. It's as if she is resigned to the fact that Sassy is gone. It's as if she's in mourning. Rachael, do you think she knows?

Yes, she has known since the day her sister left this world. She roams the rooms hoping to find her sister knowing the results will be fruitless. She does it anyway. Calling out is her way of mourning her loss; it's part of her grieving process. They (animals) are aware of life and death, and their connection to each other is a bond that cannot be understood or broken. They are of another level or dimension of reality and beyond. Hard to believe or understand, but it is as it will be, no matter what.

DEPTH OF LOVE

Rachael, why are you so good to me?

Isn't it obvious? You have no idea the depth of love that exists in this magnificent place, what you refer to as time and space. Its depth has no end. The first primary unity created was unconditional love, the first and foremost principal of life. It's what binds and unites man to woman and woman to man. That's why I'm so good to you my love. Without love nothing would exist.

I visualized you saying that with a smile.

Yes, and my eyes twinkle like the stars in God's heavens. I sing in my heart, as love in the end does conquer all.

I noticed more than once you said God's heavens, like more than one heaven?

Yes, many heavens, many rooms.

SUNSET

I sat watching the sunset,

shades of pink, gray and

violet against a soft blue sky.

The breeze lightly rustling through

the trees, and just the faintest of

melodies from the wind chimes.

And I said, "Thank you Father."

BLINK OF AN EYE

It seems as though life is flying at breakneck speed. Ten years is nothing; it's akin to the blink of an eye. When you're young you think you have all the time in the world. Boy was I wrong. I thought it would take longer to reach this age.

For those in despair and without hope life barely moves. It's as if time slows, seeming to at times stop altogether. You Kenneth are fortunate to feel as you feel. It means you're enjoying the life you have chosen within the years you have been given. Embrace your gift my love, as I will share in your joy.

THE LIFE I HAVE CHOSEN

During our last conversations Miss Rachael, you said to me "The life I have chosen." That is so unreal. Let me tell you why I say that. Many years ago I remember reading somewhere that we choose the life we are now living. So can I safely say (according to what you said) that this is true?

Partially true, most do choose their life and others are assigned their life. It's usually the younger souls that are assigned. Many being guardians learning a few valuable life lessons so they may better understand human emotions and feelings. Does that make sense to you Kenneth? Some stay long in that life, others only a short time. I myself spent many years gathering knowledge as I wandered the Earth while assigned to you. Older souls (such as yourself) have already learned much, and you could say are honing the last of their lessons.

You wandered the earth and were my guardian at the same time? How can that be?

Your secondary guardians were your main protectors as I traveled about learning the ways of the world. You were always protected, no matter what life you were in at the time. If you were between lives you were protected there also. I was always aware and vigilant as to what was going on in your life. If need be my soul-being would have come to your aid.

So what about someone, let's say a baby, dies at birth or shortly afterwards? Did they choose that life?

Possibly, but the soul knows what will be when they choose that life. The soul makes that decision knowing that they will be together with their loved ones afterwards. Remember Kenneth, I said some souls are assigned to live a life no matter how short or long it may be.

Right, I forgot. So when the parents leave and travel to the next plateau and meet that child do they know that child? And is that child still a child, or a different age?

Yes, instantaneously without any doubt whatsoever they know the child. The child is all ages, from birth to infinity. The child is all that it would be.

Wow, a bit hard to comprehend, but something for me to ponder. I'm sure many will disagree with what was spoken.

Yes they will. Think, but don't let it weigh you down in what will be.

ANOTHER RACHAEL THOUGHT

There are many things that will eventually be learned. I also have much to learn as a guardian as well as a soul. I profess to not have all the answers. I know only what is relevant to my level of consciousness. There are levels beyond my knowledge and comprehension.

AM I CRAZY?

Rachael, there are times I swear I hear Sassy cat meowing. I thought maybe it was Sissy cat, but she was nowhere to be seen. Am I crazy or is it just wishful thinking? Today is three weeks since she's gone. Am I hearing her? Is this her way of saying goodbye?

It's the totality of her love that continues to permeate your mind and heart. You hear her soft meowing as if she were still at your side. I too hear her expression of love. She loved you in life and even though you are divided by her earthly death, you are still united in the next dimension of thought and togetherness. Understand her love for you. So no Kenneth, you're not crazy. Keep in your heart her love.

280 YEARS

I remember you once mentioned you were on earth for fourteen generations. A generation is said to be twenty years. So that means you were on earth for two hundred and eighty years? Are you saying they were consecutive? How?

Yes, they were consecutive, and I left earth in 1941. Please understand, it is as it was. I entered into people's lives at opportune times and either they or I left. That's how I was able to stay that amount of time without explanation.

In 1661 it came my time to taste life as a human being. As you can imagine during my time on earth I experienced much. I tasted life, as you know it, and touched all the emotions that are placed upon mankind. I lived as both a husband and a wife, a father and a mother as to know both sides of being a parent. I was a son and a daughter, a friend and confidant. I tasted life in ways you will never know or understand, ways you would not want to know. I was of wealth, and of the lowest of poverty. I savored the sweet tones, as well as the bitter side of life. I fought in wars, and tasted famine. I was good and for a short time I touched the face of evil as to understand it. No emotion escaped my grasp; I know them all. This Kenneth is why I understand.

You didn't grow old while you were here?

No. I was of all ages. Remember nothing is impossible in my realm. We are in different dimensions. On earth you have a limited number of dimensions, but here the number is beyond great. When a child would disappear or was taken away I would appear years later as that aged child. That's only one of the many ways I was able to enter into a family. There are many circumstances that befall a family.

Isn't that cruel to the parent that you really weren't their child?

Which would you say is crueler? They never knowing what happened to that child, or being reunited and possibly fulfilling their hopes and dreams with who they believe to be their loving child? Believe Kenneth, there are outcomes in life that are far more unspeakable. Sadly they happen to this day, everyday.

Complicated, but I understand.

OTHER REALMS

I have to ask this Rachael. Why did it take you so long to come to earth to learn what you needed?

I had much to learn in other realms. I was taken to watch, guide and protect your being as you developed. Before your existence I guided others until they progressed unto their own, not needing me anymore. They advanced such as will you.

But I thought you said you would be with me forever? What about the ones you turned loose? What about them? Why aren't you going to be with them?

I will not be with them anymore. They need not of me. They will always have their other guardians. Their guardians are important insofar as having to help, guide and protect. Also, we have a choice, free will if you please to stay with whom our heart is attached. You Kenneth are my heart as well as my eternal love.

Wow, that's a thought-provoking statement.

AID

I'm sure that many times in my life you have come to my aid without my even knowing.

Oh yes Kenneth, you really kept us busy, especially when you were younger and a bit wild at times, as are many. A few times in this life, (as well as in others), your life was in real danger without you even knowing. More than once in the past you met your destiny under not the best of circumstances. So many times you took chances that could have had unfavorable outcomes with dire consequences. There are too many "I remember when" times to begin to tell you. If only you knew, and one day you will.

THANK YOU

This morning as I got out of bed I thought, "Thank you." Thank you for the aches and pains, for there are many who feel nothing. There are those unable to rise up out of bed and are confined. Thank you that I am able to walk and am not restricted in my movements. Thank you to that aging face staring back in the mirror, the one with gray hair. I am able to see and recognize that person. Thank you that I am able to think and speak without stumbling. I am able to feel and love, touch and smell. I hear the sounds of life. I have the capacity to appreciate nature and the beauty that was created for our pleasure.

Thank you. Two words with endless meaning.

GIVE AND TAKE

"Take from life what is needed, and give back for its enrichment."

SASSY CAT

Rachael, I haven't heard what I thought was Sassy Cat for a while.

She said her goodbyes, but will visit you from time to time. You may on occasion feel her presence, and her love will be with you always. Take pleasure in this; take comfort in this.

NIGHTFALL

It just stopped raining. To me there's nothing like the refreshing smell after a summer rain. It's as if the earth has been cleansed. If only.

HOPE AND INSPIRATION

Rachael, there are many who don't know what to believe as far as what's after life here on earth. Let me please share this story with them. I know you remember it well.

Yes I do. Hopefully it will give hope and inspiration, as there are many who need something in which to believe.

We have to go back to July, the year being 1995. It was five or six weeks after my father had passed from this world. My wife Mary Jo, our son Frankie and I had gone to Oscoda, a small town in Northern Michigan where we rented a cottage on Lake Huron. We were looking forward to the change, a chance to get away and do nothing special. Relax and enjoy the warmth of summer. This wasn't our first time there so we knew where to stay. We requested and got our favorite spot, cottage number five. It was right on the beach facing the lake. It had two picture windows that afforded a great view, our own slice of heaven for the week. Mary Jo would set her chair by the water and the hours would slip away as she dove into book after book. Our son Frankie would be off with new found friends from the other cabins. They would swim and play on the beach enjoying their youth and the warm summer sun. If they got tired of volleyball, or of mom and dad, they would "head down the road" to the game room. There they could play video games and drink a cola or two. I would spend my day listening to the music of Enigma, or Pink Floyd (as well as others) on my walk-man, either lying in the sun or casually walking the shoreline usually in deep thought. A well needed break. If we didn't feel like cooking, we would jump into the car and head to town for a casual dinner, which was the case most nights. Afterwards it was miniature golf, or if something good was playing we would take in a movie. A Dairy Queen would then top off our trip to town. Back to the cottage, then onto the beach to join whoever was at the fire pit that night. We would sit and talk about everything imaginable, enjoying the conversation as we sat mesmerized by the flames. One by one my fireside companions would disappear into the darkness to the warmth of their cottages. The sand was cold and damp, but the fire was there to fight off the chill of the night. Most nights ended with me sitting alone, looking at the stars and tending the campfire into the wee hours until the last of the glowing embers extinguished themselves. This was my time to be alone with my thoughts and dreams of future projects. How was I to know this night would be so extraordinary. It's as clear as if it happened yesterday.

It was late, a little before three A. M. Mary Jo and Frankie were asleep when I returned to the cottage. The night was crisp and clear and off in the distance heat lightening was flashing over the lake. I sat watching with pure enjoyment as it danced its way across the sky in bright flashes of purple and white. The storm was quite a way off, far enough that I couldn't hear any thunder.

A night to enjoy the simple pleasures of nature. It was there as I sat in the darkened cottage that I had a most unusual conversation. It was an actual conversation, not in my mind, but a spoken conversation. I was talking with someone else in the room, but the other voice was that of a spirit, not a person. It was my father. It didn't shock me, it didn't frighten me, it just happened. The conversation went much like this: "Hi Ken", and without the slightest hesitation I answered back, "Hi Dad." "I like it here", to which I replied, "That's good". "I have to go now", and I said, "Ok, I love you Dad", and he said, "I love you too". That was it. Unbelievable! Wonderful! As I sat in amazement I thought, "Why me?"

I am now thankful that it was me. Something I will always remember, it's just one of a few stories that I feel I must share. It just may give someone a shot of hope or the inspiration they need at this time.

A story worth sharing, remembering that truth is much stranger than fiction.

FAMILY

In my younger years I never fully understood or appreciated the importance of family.

Now I miss many.

FRIVOLOUS QUESTION

Rachael, I'd like to lighten up the conversation for a few moments if you please. It may seem like a frivolous question, but it's something I, as well as many others, would really like to know. It's the age-old question of how the pyramids were built?

Levitation, and no question is frivolous Kenneth.

The Egyptians knew about levitation?

Yes they did, they mastered it.

How did they learn this?

The others taught them.

The others? Who are the others and where are they from?

They were sent to help mankind learn and advance.

Who sent them and where are they from? Are they from the continent of Atlantis?

No, the people of Atlantis were a different race altogether. The others are as different as the races of today. Throughout evolution they connected with man to guide and make aware different aspects of learning. They are unique, a "one of a kind" as you would say.

You say "are" as though they still exist.

They exist, but have moved on, beyond assisting mankind on earth. I know not more of the others.

Wow, thank you.

ANOTHER DAY IN DECEMBER

Here Rachael is another story that has special meaning to me, as I'm sure it does to you also. My desire is that it gives thought to those who doubt.

I remember another special crossing that changed my life; I've had a few. It happened one day in December long ago. Years later I wrote a short story about it, titled "Another Day In December."

I think I'll always remember that day. It was a bright, crisp morning. The kind that lets you know you're in Michigan, cold, yet clear and refreshing. The snow was piled high but the sidewalks were clear, dried by the warm rays of the sun. Another day in December, just a few more then Christmas will be upon us. This day is dragging, not much business. A slow day for sure as Christmas shopping appears to have taken precedence.

I had that same dream again last night. It must be the sixth or seventh time this year. How long has it been? It must be eleven or twelve years since it first started. The same dream each time, faithful in every detail. The sandstone house with no roof, windows with no glass and a doorway without a door. In the desert, with a floor of sand, desolate. What does it mean? Next to the house is an entrance to a cave. It's made of dark, shiny stones. As I look above the entrance I see the face of Jesus; he smiles at me. Suddenly his face changes into that of Satan, and a long forked tongue comes toward me. That's it. Then I wake-up and I'm shivering, I'm cold. What does it mean? And my search for answers goes on year after year.

With nothing to do, I decide to people watch. As I looked out the window, I saw an old man walk into the street sign on the corner and fall into the snow. "Wow, he must be drunk", was my first thought. Then I noticed he was carrying a white cane with a red tip. I ran out, helped him up and brushed the snow from his tattered overcoat. No hat or gloves. He had a scratch on his brow, and a small cut on his hand. I felt sorry for this poor man. He was old, I couldn't tell his age. His hair was long and white. He had a full beard and mustache and wore thick glasses. I asked him if he was all right, and he replied that he was fine. He said, "I don't see good anymore," and asked me if I would take him to the corner store. I replied, "Yes, it's no problem." I led him to the store and he held my hand in his large, but gentle hand. He walked slowly and spoke in a soft, soothing voice. Our conversation was minimal as the store was only a few doors away. He thanked me for my kindness and walked into the store. I walked back to work, went inside and sat down. I was cold.

Christmas came early for me that year. As I sat and looked I saw a streak of blood across my palm. Without thought, instantaneously I knew it was the blood of Jesus Christ. I broke down and started to cry. My long search ended that day with that old man. For years I read, meditated, prayed and listened for the answers. At times not even knowing the questions, not knowing what I was searching for, but still searching. What to believe in? Which way to go? We all need something to believe in, something or someone to trust. The answers aren't the same for everyone, but I had my answer. I now had a path to follow; my answer was at hand. Religion! Religion was missing from my life. Not God, not faith, but religion. So simple, yet complete. I finally knew. All uncertainty left my mind. This is where the search ended and my journey began. I have to practice a religion.

I never saw that old man before that day. I knew I would never see him again, not in this lifetime. As for the dream, I never had it again. I figured out it was the fight between good and evil in me. And luckily for me evil lost.

I can only hope those who search find what they are looking for.

I must know. Was it Him Rachael?

It was He who is. It was the Messenger, and yes, it was the message.

INTUITION

Intuition may very well be your guardian angel touching
your thoughts.

GUILT

There are times, like now, when I feel guilty. Guilty I haven't done enough or that I haven't tried hard enough. I know I have always been easy on myself, not pushing hard enough to achieve some of my goals. Reaching, but not reaching higher. It may be that as I'm aging I feel remorse for things I ignored, things I should have done. I know the past cannot be changed. Do I have regrets? Yes, but only in a small way, as do many I'm sure.

I believe you're feeling melancholy at this time. All may have regrets, but you have much less than many, more than others. I must say the regrets you have are but inconsequential. These feelings are of the human condition. Hopefully you can turn this feeling into a time of reflection and learning. Take the time to think and act on your goals, as you have time enough. As the dark of night turns into the light of day, this too will just as quickly pass. My faith in you is strong my love.

BEFORE FOREVER

Rachael, you have known my soul for such a long time. As you say, "before my forever." Tell me then, how well do you know me?

Yes, I have known you before your soul came into existence. I know you to your essence, your id. I feel your truths and your untruths. I know your hopes and dreams, your likes and dislikes. Your habits as well as your idiosyncrasies, your failures and your successes as I was at your side. When you dream I feel your dream. When you touch, feel or smell, I touch, feel and smell. When you cry or are in pain, I cry as well and feel your pain. I remember every word you have ever spoken, and every iota of each life you have lived.

Your being is gentle, true and wise beyond your knowing. Your soul is old and has traveled through many lifetimes, more than even you remember. You glimpsed a few during your time in meditation. I have been there for each and every one. You hide the true self for fear of being misunderstood. Believe the day is coming when you will break out and expose the truth of your heart. Your mind and heart are of what all mankind needs to become. You are not as of yet earthly perfect, but you have enough of what is required to step into the next dimension of the one true reality. You will advance your being.

Yes Kenneth, I know you as you know not yourself. Stay true, the path will widen as you travel forward. As my words and thoughts flow I ask that you keep in yourself my trust. There is nothing I know not of you. We are interwoven, intertwined in this journey of infinite love. This Kenneth is my understanding of you.

Wow, that's more of an answer than I expected. It'll take some time to digest your words. I don't know what else to say other than I do trust you and your words. Thank you Rachael.

THE FOLLOWING NIGHT

Yes Rachael, I do have many dreams as well as passions. Listening to music tonight triggered the following thought. I pursue at least two passions that to me are meaningful expressions of what I see, feel and think. One being painting, the act of creating an image not before seen, something out of my mind. The other being the written word, which possesses power beyond belief. They both are capable of transporting you to wondrous places. They can lift you; or bring tears of joy or despair. They raise your being to the highest of high, or transport you into the depths of your very self. These are truly gifts from God. There are many masters of these disciplines. I profess not to be a master, just a creature of life following my heart and mind.

Well said Kenneth, as passion truly is a gift to be cherished, and these gifts are meant to be shared.

THE RIGHT CHOICES

I can only hope as I go through life I make the right choices. And if I choose wrong, remember that I'm doing the best I can. So please, don't judge me, and let's not judge one another.

A DAY TO REMEMBER

Rachael, there is something I must know of you. Some years ago when I was working I had something happen to me and the outcome was nothing short of a miracle. Before I pose my question, let me refresh your memory of the events on that day.

As remodeling work was being done, Travis (a maintenance co-worker) and I were in charge of cutting down and removing all old electrical conduit and unnecessary ironwork. The electrician in charge of that aspect of the job had disconnected all unnecessary power. I was in a lift (about twenty feet in the air) cutting conduit with a cutting torch when I hit a 250-volt direct current line that was not disconnected. Not a good thing. According to Travis, a flame shot out from the line that encompassed a six-foot or larger area. I dropped the torch and started patting myself to put out the fire. Surely my clothing had to be on fire. To my great surprise nothing was burning and I was totally unharmed. Nothing, no electrical burns or burns from the flame. A true miracle if ever there was one.

So Miss Rachael, tell me what you know of that day.

A day to remember, a day of learning. We were all there to protect you my love. Favor was with you as my cloak encompassed you; sheltering you from the flaming harm as your other guardians fought the electrical voltage surging within. It was for you a truly dangerous situation brought about by others not prudent in their responsibilities. But all ended well my love.

Yes Rachael, all ended well that day. I can't remember if it was the same day or the following day when we continued our task. I do remember telling Travis that if I didn't continue cutting I would never get over what happened. He agreed and I got into the lift to begin. I encountered something new that day. As I prepared to start cutting I broke out in a cold sweat and noticed an odor unfamiliar to me. It was strong and pungent, an overwhelming smell and my olfactory senses were working overtime. Only later did I realize what I was experiencing. It was fear, I was smelling fear. Yes, a day to remember. I thank you and the other guardians for protecting and keeping me from harm.

(A Rachael smile)

EINSTEIN

It is said that Einstein used a small percentage of his brain, and most other people use even less. Is that true? And how much do we really use?

Most use all of it, but not all at once. Many believe this not to be so. Believe, as it is so. It is in constant motion evolving to the point of unity with all of all, attempting to unite mind, body and spirit. It is reaching to elevate itself into the winds of all that is universal. With some it becomes corrupt and poisoned. There are those who are misled and control not their own mind and destiny. They are in need of redemption. The time is nearing for resolution when man and woman must atone for the actions of their lives. Stay vigil and on the road to truth and light. Use it wisely. Stay aware.

Wow, its strange how one thought connects to another.

This is the mind doing what it does.

LAWS OF THE UNIVERSE

I've noticed many of our conversations have similar, or at times, the same conclusions. Does this seem strange to you or would you say it's only a coincidence?

What I say Kenneth is what I say. Events are governed by the laws of the universe of God and of what will be. No matter if the seeking question is the same or not, the answer is as it will be. Nothing different, nothing more. Accept what is and enjoy what is given. Enjoy what you possess, what you are and what you believe. Believe that all is possible, and one day you will marvel in the grandeur of what is given. Do not question with skepticism but open your mind to what can and will be, of what is and what will be, of now and what will be forever.

It is said that all roads lead to Rome, the truth being all roads lead to an unbelievable existence beyond what you can fathom. Believe and trust. That's all I ask my dear Kenneth.

ABOUT A DOG

Earlier tonight I read a story that touched my heart. It was about a dog and it brought me to tears. It brought back thoughts of my loving Sassy cat. I miss her so much. Please send her spirit to me tonight as I sleep so I can see her and touch her again, if only in my dreams. I miss her purring and the nose kisses she gave me in the morning when I first woke. Please.

Be silent this night; listen and feel with your heart.

DESTINY

Here's something I have thought about many times my dear Rachael. Can you change your destiny?

Your destiny is your destiny. You can however alter the events leading to the one of many. Ultimately my dear Kenneth, your destiny is that of your choosing.

If it's one of many how can it be my destiny? How can that be?

By changing your mindset, thinking and asking the universal mind to be your guide. Take the path you normally would reject. Ask, then open your being and receive the guidance offered you. These changes will decide your final destiny. It is all there, waiting for you to command what will be. It may be unknown to you as how to clear your thoughts and connect to this great power. Give not up as you undertake this endeavor. Think, try and then do. It is within your grasp, it is attainable. One thing more, remember this, change and choice will alter your outcome. It is of your choosing. It is free will.

I'm not sure I understand.

Think of what I have spoken; open your mind then you will understand

RACHAEL'S WORDS

There are things that take lifetimes to accomplish. You may not be able to finish all that you wish in one lifetime. Patience.

SECRETS

I already know the answer, but I'm going to ask regardless. Rachael, you're not divulging earth-shattering secrets, or telling me things I shouldn't know, are you?

(Chuckle) No Kenneth, I have much knowledge but no secrets here. Some know and have known everything we talk about, and more. We have merely scratched the surface of what is to be taught, and what is to be learned. If only people took empty time to quiet the self, and open entirely to what is already there. So much knowledge and wisdom available to anyone willing to search the recesses of their mind. If only they would stop wasting precious moments on superfluous thoughts and actions. Time is not replaceable and should be used wisely. Think how much better the world would be if we collectively spent time in meditation, prayer and positive thinking. This would lead to positive actions, and positive actions would lead to the betterment of all mankind. No Kenneth, no secrets here, only truths.

A NEW DAY

Rachael, I've been thinking about what's going on in the world. It seems to be on the edge of insanity. I hope that one day this will be a world at peace. So I ask this, will this world ever be at peace?

I know what I know. Dawn of the new day will bring peace and harmony to your world, with or without man.

STOP AND LISTEN

It seems that for the past few days I once again am having a hard time getting it together. I wish I knew why.

Sometimes when you push too hard you need to stop and relax. Pray for strength. Stop and listen. Be at peace within. Give thanks for what is. Just stop, breath and enjoy what has been given. Love and be at peace in your mind, heart and self. Smile Kenneth, as I love you.

Thank you Rachael.

SEASONS

The seasons are changing and autumn is upon us. I also am in the season of my autumn. Rachael, do you know when my spirit will leave this earthly body and embark onto the next phase of my journey?

I know what I know. I am bound to speak not of the time of your transition. It is not important for you to know. What is important is you have much time to love and create what will be shown. The natural beauty provided you and the world is to be appreciated, to be a joy to your senses. Live your life, love your life. Live in the season, enjoy the season. You once stated, "Enjoy life. Don't spend an excessive amount of time worrying about dying. It will happen in due course." Listen to your words.

A PERSONAL THOUGHT

I have been here many years and my thinking seems to have shifted. I believe this shift took place longer ago than I realized. If this happens to all, I don't know. I know I see things with eyes that are older, yet clearer. I hear with different intentions. I learned from those close to me, and from those I love. I am ultimately different and still evolving as my time progresses and believe life should be lived as best one is able. We are all on a different path, but the journey leads to the same destination. If you believe, or if you don't, one day each and every one of us will know. Earthly death is the ultimate life (as we know life) adventure. I look forward to the advancement but feel I am not ready to take that step, although the timing is not of our choosing in most cases. So I will bide my time, experience and enjoy as much as I am able. And when my time comes I can only hope I will be ready.

When you are ready fear not, as I will be there with you. (Smile)

Once again, thank you Rachael for your reassuring words.

THIRD RACHAEL THOUGHT

I cannot tell you everything, but I can help you remember the past.

DÉJÀ VU

You know how one thought leads to another, then another? I was thinking about something (can't remember what) and my thought process took me to this question for you my dear Rachael. What can you tell me about déjà vu?

Well my dear Kenneth, here's what I can tell you about déjà vu. It's not a mystery. In fact it's reasonably simple. The same thought process that connects one thought to another is somewhat how dejavu works. The mind records every experience, every thought and word you have ever experienced and said. As your experiences overlap they present to you something that seems to have happened at another time in your life, when in fact it may be the first time. Also, it could be a repeat of an earlier time, a previous life. All the experiences of each life carry forward with your soul. When one life comes to an end and everything stops, that's not the end. It's a stepping-stone to the next existence.

Everything is energy, everything, and you cannot destroy energy. It goes on forever. That being said, your energy goes with you into your next phase of being. So at times it may well have happened before and you're having a flashback of another time. That's it, reasonably simple. I must add that of all energy, the greatest is love. In the being of being, love is the way, love is the answer. Without love you are lost. I hope that helps answer your question my love.

Thank you Rachael, a sufficient answer.

SISTERS

Earlier in the year I had something unusual happen to me. It was morning and I was laying in bed going over in my mind what was on my agenda for the day. As I lay there I felt two pokes on my arm, one after the other. It didn't frighten me Rachael, but I was wondering who it was?

I remember Kenneth, it was your sister.

Beverly?

No, it was your other sister, Sandra.

Wow, for some reason I would have thought Beverly when you said it was my sister. Why did she poke me, do you know?

Yes, she wanted to thank you for being there and caring. She really loves you more than you realize. That was her way of saying thank you. Remember when she intervened and saved your life? If she had not been there your young life would have ended that fateful day. That was an incident that changed your life's outcome. It's what I was talking about when we talked about changing your destiny. In that instance, your sister, not you, changed it.

If she hadn't been here that day, I wouldn't be here today. I wish I would have known who it was when it happened.

You know now, take comfort in that.

You're right Rachael, I will take comfort in knowing. Thank you.

KARMA

Earlier this week we spoke of déjà vu. Somehow it led me to think about karma. I'm not sure why, but maybe I see them in the same realm of possibilities. Rachael, enlighten me on your perception of karma if you please.

What can I tell you other than karma does exist. There are many who believe not (or choose not) in karma and of its affects. Many learn the truth the hard way and suffer the consequences of karma. Only then do they possibly believe and understand how it works. As with déjà vu, it travels with you from life to life. What you pay not for in this life, you pay for in another. In the end karma happens, there is no escaping its affects. People would be more careful if they truly knew how karma may well change things. The price may be greater than most may be willing to pay. So it would be wise to think before you act.

Good advice Rachael.

TALENT

Recently a friend and I were talking about painting. Later that evening I started thinking about talent. You look around and you realize there are so many talented people in the world. In just your small circle of life this can be seen. It made me wonder if everyone has a talent of sorts. Rachael, does everyone have a talent?

Yes Kenneth, I tell you that everyone has some unique quality or talent. Many possess more than one. You may find this hard to believe, but believe when I say everyone. Many may seem not to and that may be a loss on their part. They may never have searched for that special gift, or ever realize they possess such a gift. Remember too that talent comes in many forms. Some may paint, such as you, or dance, play an instrument, or tailor clothing. They may have the ability to prepare food, or sing with the voice of an angel (no pun intended) or one of many other talents. A person may have the special ability to nurture or comfort the sick and dying. Mother Teresa was a good example of such a person, kind, compassionate and totally giving of herself. As we speak, she is being considered for sainthood, and many would tell you she is already a saint. All a person needs to do my dear Kenneth is look within. Look within and you will find that special talent, the gift. It is a part of your life's purpose, that thing that excites your heart and gives you reason to smile.

So some people never find their talent, and others are considered masters or best in their field. What's that all about? How does that come about Rachael?

You at times see child prodigies and wonder how is this possible. What you learn in one life carries on with you in all your lifetimes. Its no different than karma, it is carried forward with you. As with anything, the more you do the better you become. Only when it's ready to reveal itself does it emerge from within. A genius or child prodigy may be the culmination of previous lifetimes finally exploding in the form of greatness. We all have the capability to become that person. At times new souls have that spark of genius. I cannot explain how that is, as I know not. After all that I have said, please remember this Kenneth; greatness can be measured in small feats of every day life. Just look with an open mind and your heart will see.

UNHOLY KARMA

We talk about love and all the good in the world, but what about the bad things that happen in the world and the evil people who perform these acts?

Even before the appearance of man on earth evil existed. There is much unholy karma in the lineage of these demons. Many are nothing more than pure evil personified. Many people choose to not believe in the powers of evil. Believe, as these forces are in constant motion in all places and at all times. They not only prey upon the innocent and on the weak of mind, but anywhere they have an entrance. They never sleep. They are relentless in their unholy effort. It is the ying and the yang. Be heedful, as are your guardians, always present and always vigilant. You understand what I say is in action.

I will be mindful.

THE WORLD

The world is a great place, and at the same time it's shameful what mankind is doing to it, as well as to each other.

MY GUARDIANS

I was thinking about something you mentioned earlier in one of our conversations. Correct me if I'm wrong, but I believe you spoke of other guardians beside yourself. Tell me of them, if you please.

Well Kenneth, besides your family members you have three other guardians, two females and one male. The male is the youngest and is just starting his time of learning. The two young ladies, if you will, have been with you for some time now and are well versed in their charge. They are really super guardians, as you might say. So my dear Kenneth, you are well protected.

And am I to believe they have names?

Sorry, yes they do. The girls answer to the names of Karoll and Emmaleen. And the youngster is called Zarya.

Thank you Rachael. I will rest well.

———————◄►———————

WINGS

I often wondered if angels have wings as you always see them depicted that way. You once mentioned your cloak but never said anything about wings. Is this a silly question Rachael?

Well, no we really don't have wings as they appear. And no, not a silly question. What we do have is a cloak, which appears to be, or resemble, wings. You more than once had the protection of my, as well as the others, cloak envelop you without ever knowing or feeling. Know you were more than once being protected from certain danger Kenneth. Even though they appear as wings, no Kenneth, no wings. (Smile)

Interesting bit of information, thanks once again.

DEATH AND NEAR DEATH

Rachael, just recently I watched a movie about a near-death experience. I've read several books on the subject and am wondering how this works?

As you must know, near death and actual death have different outcomes. There are different scenarios when your life on earth is no longer. Ultimately they all lead to the same ending, which is absolute love. Pure love. If only you knew the power of a pure and total love. It is wholly consuming with feelings that I cannot begin to describe. It must be experienced, felt to understand of what I speak.

Believe when I say to you my dear Kenneth, you will one day know of what I speak. Place in me your trust, as I will help guide you when your time comes. This is all you need to know for now.

And what of the people who don't believe in God or an afterlife? What about them?

They will learn and know what is truth. They will know God and all his mercy, and of His majesty.

I put my trust in you Rachael.

(A smile from Rachael)

MISSING YOU

Today is my Mom's birthday. She was born in Detroit on a Friday, the 27th of October 1916. "Friday's child is loving and giving." I love and miss you Mom.

SPECIAL PEOPLE

Special needs people touch many families, including mine. What about them Rachael, what can you tell me of them?

They receive special attention and admiration in heaven for their challenging time on earth. It was their choice, as they may have had a lesson to learn, or perhaps to teach. A part may well have been missing in their total earthly or heavenly development. It may not seem that they would learn, being in their somewhat locked life, but many lessons are to be learned no matter the circumstances. Hard to believe I am sure for you. Also, they do enjoy their life more than would be expected even though at times it is quite trying. When they leave their earthly body they advance faster, like going to the front of the line. They are as they are meant to be, perfect in every way, no imperfections as when they were on earth. You are all special in the eyes of God, but they have a slight edge, as do the young children. They are not to be pitied; they are to be loved, as are all living creatures. All of mankind and all of heaven respond to love. I must tell you the structure here is what it is, fair, unlike events on earth, but could be considered a paradox in your world. You on your special day will understand of what I speak, as will all inhabitants of your world.

This can very well help many who live with special people, just in knowing all is and will be well. Thank you Rachael, for once again you have opened my eyes as well as my mind. My heart has already been opened.

REFOCUS

Rachael, well here I am again, procrastinating. It seems the last two or three days has my mind in shut down mode. Or maybe I'm just being lazy or easy on myself.

Well Kenneth, I feel as if you're just a little tired. Maybe you need these few days to get refocused. I know you, and I know you will once again move forward. Remember to start your day with your daily reading of inspiration. You haven't read it in a few days and I know that always nudges you into action. Don't be too hard on yourself. I will help push you, as it were, into action. Smile, I still love you. (Smile)

Thanks Rachael, I need a push every so often.

Yes.

CHOICES AGAIN

Sometimes I look around and know that life can be so unfair. Just watch the news daily and you will see what I say is true. I remember my sister once telling my mother that she seems not to care what was happening in the world; the hate, murder and personal tragedy that befall people. My mothers response was somewhat like this, "I know what's happening in the world. I choose not to let it upset me, as I am unable to change the things that befall others. So I choose not to dwell on these matters." What are your thoughts Rachael?

Once again it comes to choice, and your mother made a choice. Her words are truth. Life is life. There are times when you can have great influence on a matter, and other times you can do not a thing to change the outcome. If you cannot alter the result, then you must accept what is. What more can I tell you.

LESSONS

After a conversation with a friend a thought was triggered. It was of a person who was close to me at one time. She is now gone from this earth, but still with me in my mind and heart. After an ill-fated event she told me that nothing mattered to her anymore. I truly believe she had given up. As time went on she never seemed the same and at the end I feel she was tired of this life. Knowing her life I can understand where she was coming from. Sad, but true. At times her life was exciting, adventurous and troubling all mixed into her years. Many loved her, yet at times others used her, often willingly known by her. She was always for the underdog, and time after time this proved to bring about problems. Her good intentions often backfired. Always seeking for what was never to be, never. And yet it was the simplest of requests, nothing more than to be accepted. Life is a paradox. What more can I say, it needs no explanation. She will always be in my mind and heart.

Yes, such at times is life. Many lessons to be experienced and learned. Know that she has and is still learning and smiling now with thoughts of you. She truly loves you, and the love you have for each other transcends time and distance. Your journey will, with her, one day again continue in the cosmos. Time is not of importance; love is what matters. Love and trust one another. I understand you miss her, but you have a special bond that cannot be broken, not even by her earthly death. Love her as she loves you my dear Kenneth. Smile with her thoughts.

Thanks Rachael (smile)

WHY ME?

Rachael, I am going to assume that you picked me. So then I must ask, why did you pick me?

My dear Kenneth, there are many reasons why I picked you. As you were being formed is when my heart went to you. I fell in love with your spirit, and your smile. Your soul touched me with unbelievable love. I admired and respected the honesty of your heart. Besides, I like brown eyes. (Chuckle) I love what you are to become, your ultimate transformation is the culmination of all your life trials and tribulations. All your different lifetimes shape you into the true you. You are a teacher of the future and many will learn of your insights far after your life journey on earth is finished. You are a true being of the true ones. That's why my dear Kenneth.

You're embarrassing me Rachael.

This is how I feel and why I picked you. Remember, you asked.

Touché.

MORNING LIGHT

I miss my family Rachael. I miss my sisters, my mom and dad, nephew and aunts. I miss them all. Guess I'm in a sentimental mood or something. It could be as I'm a bit tired and somewhat set aback by a recent event. And no, I don't feel like going into details. No elaborations, if you please. Anyway, you know the details.

Rest well tonight my Kenneth. The morning light will be bright and you will see anew. Believe.

HIS CHILDREN

There are times when, even at my age, I act or think like a little kid. Most likely everyone does at one time or another. I can't be the only one. I hope not anyway.

I believe you're not the only adult who acts like a child every now and then. The innocence of a child is a beautiful thing to behold. Believe this Kenneth, we are all His children. Yes, I said "we."

Even you Rachael? And all the others guardians?

Yes, even me and all the others guardians.

GOD AND LOVE

Rachael it seems like many of our conversations end or talk about God and love. Some might say I have an agenda, which is not the case, as our conversations are spontaneous. I speak of things that interest me, and am curious as to what answer you will present. No agenda pushing here. What do you think?

Remember earlier I said to you, "People will think what they will think no matter what." Worry not what the naysayer says, trust in my words. Many do believe and know that God and love are the answer. The one answer that can change the direction of your world. Believe this Kenneth, many at this time are on the destructive path and must change if they are to be saved. Prayer does work, especially when done by multitudes. Believe and pray. Trust my words and the truth in your heart Kenneth.

You know I trust you Rachael.

FAITH

Rachael, you know what I have been thinking the last few days. I do not have to share the details or even the thoughts with you. But you know my feelings and I am afraid of what I am thinking.

Kenneth, I say believe in what I told you. Please have faith in my words and all will be well.

It's hard Rachael, even though I believe your words I will meditate and pray on this. I just need a sign, or maybe my faith is weak at this time.

I have answered you, now believe. Please. Set you mind at ease so that you may continue to thrive and create things of beauty and wonder. Please Kenneth.

Thank you Rachael.

DOUBT

More than once I have thought about death and dying. I profess not to be fearful of death, but then I wonder if I am? It's an easy thing to say, being I'm not staring at death directly. Maybe I'm not afraid to die; it's just the unknown way of reaching the afterlife that bothers me a bit. Sooner or later we all come to the realization that one day we will be in the afterlife and face what to many is the unknown. My point, I don't know. Maybe it's just that we all have doubt at one time or another. I believe in the afterlife and can only hope it's as good as I believe it will be.

Well Kenneth, it's better than you can ever imagine. All have doubt at one time or another. Some believe, others that nothing exists after death. They will be so surprised. Your thought was, "Will I remember the afterlife once I am there and if I decide to come back?" No, once you come back all memory of paradise are beyond memory. A few have glimpsed its interior and returned to speak of it somewhat. They know not of the full grandeur. Heaven is for heaven, and not to be shared in its true majesty, not until you enter its realm once again, totally. It may seem selfish, but it is as it is, as it was designed. There is reason for everything. Trust and believe, and at the end of your earthly visit you will see the truth of what I speak. (A Rachael smile)

A LIVING SUPERCOMPUTER

Here's a thought. At times I have such bizarre thoughts, and in a minute I'll tell you what prompted this question.

Well, the mind is a complex and wondrous functioning mechanism, a living supercomputer in your terms. It is capable of extraordinary measures. It can generate random thoughts, from there connecting to thoughts long ago forgotten and others in now time. You can take control, or by letting loose the mind can lead you to exciting happenings. Try it, as you did in meditation. Take yourself to the outer limits of reality, onto the edge of that which is future.

Earlier I asked what we could talk about? The answer I got was, "Fire, water and air." The elements of earth, which I thought somewhat strange. Through synapse connections, your answer somehow leads me to wonder, "Why were animals created?

Animals were created for many reasons, one being to provide a variety of food for mankind. Domestic animals such as sheep, cattle, chicken and such provide sustenance for man along with fruits, nuts and vegetables. As far as so-called wild animals, they were created for balance and for this simple fact: that fact being for His pleasure. The pleasure of pure beauty and diversity.

Balance? His pleasure?

Yes, balance, and simply for His pleasure. He enjoys the beauty He created and wants to share these magnificent creatures with mankind.

Balance as to control and prevent overpopulation of one creature over another. If left unchecked the one could upset the balance of nature, and the collapse of nature possibly would occur. So balance.

Now Kenneth, do you see how the mind can work?

Yes, and this is another something I will have to think about.

———————————

LOOK ABOUT AND SEE

Of the many skylines in this world,
many I have seen, many I have not.
Which would be deemed the most
breathtaking that is of course?

Possibly the harbor at Sydney,
or the Eiffel of France.
Perhaps Singapore or Hong Kong,
would they obtain your vote?

Surely many deserve our consideration.

These few would be my picks.
Some I have seen, some I have not.
The Himalayas of course,
with thoughts of Shambala

Mount Kilimanjaro for sure,
the mountain called Tabletop another.
Magnificent to say the least,
nature's skylines extraordinaire.

The work of God at its finest.

ANOTHER STORY

I have a story for you Rachael. I know you remember it well, probably in more detail than I can remember.

I know what story this is, but go ahead Kenneth. Please tell, as I want to see how well you remember that night those long years ago.

I guess Mary Jo and I had been married a little over a year when we moved into an apartment. We were in the process of decorating and I was hanging the window shades. I was on the stepladder, Mary Jo would hand the shades to me and I would install them. I remember sitting on the top step, which is a no-no, and a big mistake. While reaching and sort of twisted backwards to finish hanging the shade I started falling backward off the ladder. I was beyond the point of no return when something propelled me forward to an upright position preventing me from falling. An unexplained force saving me from an unhealthy outcome. I'm sure it would have been an unpleasant event had I hit the floor from that height.

I never thought much about what saved me that day, but now I have a suspicion that you had something to do with it. So am I correct in thinking this Rachael?

Yes, I couldn't let you fall Kenneth. I love you too much to let something that simple befall you. I am here to protect you as best I am allowed, as you are my charge. I was also the force stopping you from going too far forward and possibly falling face first. Your heart was beating so fast, and you broke out in a cold sweat. You were both shook up, but you were without harm. I remember that day well.

So now after all these years, I know what saved me. It was you Rachael, and I thank you once again for protecting me from myself. (Smile)

FOREVER

Forever is a concept that is truly hard to grasp. So I ask this Rachael, will everything go on forever, or will it come to an end?

Everything that you know of now will end, but all else will go on forever.

FAMILY MEMBERS

I just thought of something else you mentioned in an earlier conversation. Family members are also guardian angels, correct? Tell me who my family guardians are if you please.

All your family members are guardians at one time or another. It just depends on the situation and circumstances of what's happening in your life.

I understand, thank you.

ONE MORE THING

There is one more thing I would like to know, but I hesitate to ask at this time. It has to be presented in the right context, so maybe I should save it for future conversations. Yes, that's what I'll do.

You will know when it is time to learn what is to be answered. Only then will it be asked, only then will it be answered.

QUESTION

Sitting in the dark listening to my music, this thought came into my mind. A thought not directed at anyone special, but just a thought.

Were you there?
Did you witness it?
Did you weep at His feet?
Were you there when the heavens opened?
Were you there when they wept for the Lord of Lords?
Were you there when God the Father welcomed His Son into eternal life?
Were you there?

LAST CONVERSATION FOR NOW

Rachael, these last months have opened my eyes a bit wider. You expanded my mind, and told me things that touched my heart. You changed my way of thinking about the many elements of life. You nudged my memory during these conversations, tasting sweet times from the past, and touching times of sorrow and despair. You took me into the future of what will be, and inspired me to look, to see and to move forward. You have done things for me that I did not do for myself. You know of what I speak.

So I say thank you Rachael, and I look forward to our future conversations, as I know they will be many.

We have just started on your path of what is to come. Be patient and rest well my love.

TIME TO REFLECT

It is time I stop so as to absorb and reflect on the words spoken. The end of our conversations for now, but possibly the beginning of your own...

THE END

www.ingramcontent.com/pod-product-compliance
Lightning Source LLC
Chambersburg PA
CBHW032011040426
42448CB00006B/582